ETSY BUSINESS FOR BEGINNERS

HOW TO BUILD & PROMOTE A PROFITABLE ETSY BUSINESS

Devon Wilcox

ClydeBank
·MEDIA

Copyright © 2014
ClydeBank Media
All Rights Reserved

ISBN-13 : 978-1507546895

CONTENTS

INTRODUCTION

From homemade candles to handmade pillows, Etsy is the primary online marketplace for those who are looking for something not be typically found at a big box store. Items that are unique, have lots of character, and are defined by their originality dominate the Etsy world. It is what makes the site so different from all the other retailers. In order to profit from items that result from a hobby, or some vintage ornaments from your grandparent's basement, you used to have to sell them at a garage sale or flea market. The introduction of Etsy now allows those same items to reach a global customer base with just a few simple clicks.

Etsy advances the growing movement away from mass produced commercial products to more personal and unique work that is shifting consumer preferences across the world. Through this website, one can set up their shop, list their products for sale, and reach a global client base in a matter of minutes. Since it is so easy to set up and get started, it is critical to differentiate yourself from the crowd to stand head and shoulders above your competition. In order to do this, you must understand how to create products that speak to your intended target audience, market your offerings so that they drive huge traffic to your storefront, and provide exceptional customer service so that your customers will keep coming back for more.

This book will teach you everything you need to know in order to build and maintain a profitable profile that will allow you to turn those vintage items or your hand knit scarves into real money. This step-by-step guide will show you exactly what you need to know, from making your first sale on Etsy to deciding what type of business organization you should form. Nothing beats hard work and determination, but coupled with the knowledge and strategies in this book, you will be so successful on Etsy that you will wish you had started sooner.

Welcome to the first day of the rest of your life.

CHAPTER ONE
What is Etsy? and How To Use This Book

Etsy is an electronic marketplace that facilitates a connection between buyers and sellers. You can buy or sell three types of producs on Etsy: handmade items, vintage items that are over 20 years old, or supplies to make or refurbish the first two. Right away, you'll notice that there is something different about this site. Because of this difference, you might want to think about ways to engage the marketplace and the people who frequent it. You should take note that Etsy buyers spend a lot of money on stores hosted at the site. The question you should ask yourself is: What can be my share of Etsy's success?

Anyone can log on to Etsy, browse through the site, pick out a name and open up a storefront. Quite quickly you will come across a store selling items that you might very well make at home as a hobby or in your spare time. You may be a great seamstress or really handy with knitting needles. The next step is to take this skills and apply them to the Etsy platform to get a piece of that audience. This book will walk you through exactly how to become a thriving part of the Etsy culture.

How to Use This Book

To make the most out of the information in this book, follow these steps to ensure that reading this book will be most beneficial to your journey toward becoming a successful Etsy seller:

1. Know About the World of Etsy

Chapter One briefly covers what Etsy is all about and how you can make your mark in it as a hobbyist, handicrafter, or marketing person.

2. Determine What You Can Offer to the Growing Market of Etsy

Etsy is comprised of more than 800,000 creative entrepreneurs catering to more than 20 million registered users around the world. Chapter Two will help you determine in what niche you can base your shop and take advantage of market demands.

3. The Nitty-Gritty of Product Selling

In Chapter Three, the basics of product pricing will be discussed to ensure profits in your Etsy shop. You need to know these tips to make sure that you are not burning resources and that you are ensuring positive returns to your business.

4. Develop Your Etsy Selling Skills

Chapter Four talks about understanding the Etsy marketplace. You need to know what your customers want and how you can deliver particular products. From product research, creation, promotions, search engine optimization, and social media marketing strategies, you will get tips you need to succeed in this chapter.

5. Establishing Your Etsy Business

Chapter Five discusses how to establish your business by making a business plan and completing business registration forms. The chapter makes the process of business registration easier to understand.

6. Making Your Shop Successful

Chapter Six provides important tips and tricks to making and keeping your Etsy shop successful. This chapter helps you understand the importance of creating good listings and working with customers. The crucial thing to remember is that once you have your shop up and running, you aren't done; you have only begun the real work!

7. Learn from the Pros

Chapter Seven contains case studies of Etsy powersellers, which will inspire you to push through if the going gets tough. These powersellers are living testimonies showing thatyou can succeed as well – doing what you love and living your dreams.

CHAPTER TWO
Developing The Project Blueprint

Handmade

You can think of homemade in terms of arts and crafts or something you would have made in a high school shop class, but it doesn't stop there. It can be anything you make at home: whether it's seashell art, decorative items, fine art, sculptures, jewelry, knitted or crochet clothing. You could, for instance, find a niche in wedding knick-knacks. As long as you made it at home, it is completely welcome to be sold on Etsy. Open yourself up creatively and think outside the box. The possibilities are endless. Authenticity is important; if Etsy administrators find that your product is factory made or mass produced, your account will be shutdown.

Vintage

This is the perfect category for someone who isn't particularly skilled in the hands-on or creative work. There was some controversy and misunderstanding over what defines the term, "vintage." Etsy has clarified it to mean anything that is more than 20 years old. Vintage products can follow the old adage of "one man's junk is another man's treasure." You should spend a good amount of time familiarizing yourself with what is currently listed for sale on Etsy to get an idea of the supply and demand in this category. Visit garage sales, your grandmother's attic, your uncle's old barn, local antique shops and thrift stores. You never know what you might find, and it just might be profitable.

Supplies

Everything from paper and scissors to wood and nails can be sold and purchased here. Instead of taking money out of the Etsy system and buying supplies elsewhere, you can purchase these items in the same pool. Not only is keeping currency within the Etsy system a well thought out business strategy, but it is a great convenience for buyers and sellers are concerned.

Prohibited Items

Etsy does have a few rules about what can't be sold on their website. We've discussed what you can sell, but let's take a brief moment and discuss what you can't sell. Visit https://www.etsy.com/help/article/4525 to view the complete list of prohibited merchandise. Etsy says that these items aren't in the spirit of what they are trying to do and offer, and that is why these sales are prohibited on the website. If someone does try to sell prohibited items through Etsy, the listing will be taken down by the administration. If violations persist or are serious enough, Etsy will close down your shop and account.

The Edge

Remember you are selling to a group of people who are used to finding unique or handmade items that are of good quality. You can't imitate something; you must make it your own and let the marketplace see that., In addition to the physical product, what you are selling is a dimension of personality for which buyers are willing to fork out a little extra. They are not interested in something commercially born and bred. Make something unique by hand or find a profitable treasure. Do not mistake Etsy for eBay or any other e-commerce website. You need to include a certain amount of character in the product before it takes off. The edge is individuality.

Being successful on Etsy is like doing the waltz. It takes two to dance, and it is a graceful display of unity. Deciding what to make, and actually creating your piece is a harmonious blend of your craft and your final product. Together, you and your products perform a graceful display of artistic ideal. When you can strike the right beat, you and your product will hit stardom.

CHAPTER THREE

Products & Pricing

Product

The product refers to anything you place in your store. The selection of the product, or the product mix, is what you're going to sell. Keep in mind that you can sell various types of products, but don't limit yourself to just one niche. You may want to give this area a significant amount of thought. By using Etsy, you are opening yourself up to a huge market. You are not necessarily limited to the visitors on Etsy, but you are also able to sell to the world at large. Etsy gives you a base to begin your online operations. You need to visualize your product in three dimensions: the range of products you offer, the depth of those products, and variations you can customize if needed. Defining your product offering is a significant step towards becoming successful on Etsy.

Range and Depth of Products

Whatever your selected niche is, make sure you're providing a unique and wide range of items within your category. For instance, if you have a store containing items for weddings, you should have a wide variety within that category to reflect that. For example: invitation cards, guest books, centerpieces, etcetera. You could even have customized handmade plaques with engraved vows. Capitalizing on something unique will set you apart from others with the same niche.

Creativity is key. You should always strive to keep expanding and creating a brand for yourself; never be afraid to do too much. Add to your range of products as you look into ways in which you can create variations of existing products. Think about using different colors, materials, fonts, sizes, pages, and textures. Keep in mind the more options your buyers have, the more likely they are to find something they want. Do not hesitate to go through the details of what your customer envisions and then, if necessary, send them a free sample.

Pricing Strategies

There are a number of philosophies on pricing strategies at Etsy. The pricing strategies are dependent upon the product and the buyer. More often than not, buyers are more interested in quality. Because handmade items are a premium, do not sell yourself short. When defining price points, first pay attention to the "going-rate" for your particular item. Second, note the quantity of like items already available on Etsy. Last, the quality of those items versus your own product should determine your price point.

1. Cost Plus Price

Cost plus refers to a certain percentage above the total cost of raw materials and the cost of the time it takes you to make the product. Your profit results after accounting for all the costs to make the product. It is not just the cost of all the raw materials it takes to make the product, but also the fixed costs that go in to it. If you are making wedding bands, the cost includes the material to make the bands, the cost to engrave them, and the cost of the shipping box and packing materials. Take note that the above is just the direct cost. You also have to include the cost of any space you rent to house all your equipment. If you make one product a year, you need to include 12 months of rental and utilities into your cost. Once you add both . If you have no other income, you need to include the amount of funds that would allow you to sustain yourself over the course of the production. Once you have this cost breakdown, you have an idea of the bare minimum you can charge for your product.

If you need a more convenient tool to determine the price of your product, check out this free Etsy calculator. It helps you determine the right price for your product by calculating shipping price, discount, cost per item, advertising cost, desired profit, and other costs. Etsy Pricing Calculator is a handy tool for many Etsy sellers, and you should may also find it helpful in your operations.

2. Market Price

Market price is based on what the market will bear. This usually starts out at a high price and works its way down to the point when it meets the demand of the market. This kind of pricing is risky in the sense that it might turn off customers who may deem your product too expensive, causing them to move on to other products.

3. Competitive Pricing

The third method is competitive pricing. Here, you price your products according to similar products on Etsy. By understanding the competition, you will determine your product's price. If you find that your cost exceeds prices that your competitors are charging, , you need to rethink the production and reduce your indirect cost. You can either go slightly higher or go slightly lower. If you go slightly higher, you put yourself in the premium market by saying that your artistic talent is more valuable. If you believe this, do so. If you price your product lower, you are benchmarkingDecide how to position yourself in the pricing field.

4. Combination Pricing

The fourth pricing method is a combination method, where you price your offerings across a wide scope. You can have a range of specific products that are presented towards the premium market, as well as products that are priced lower. The benefit of combination pricing can be enormous, especially if you have wide range and a deep offering. When this is the case, you can cater to more people.

Pricing a Brand vs. Pricing a Product

When you price a single product, you can use a simple strategy, namely the first to third methods listed above. However, when you price a brand, you have to change your frame of mind. Pricing a brand is done with a higher degree of purpose and vision. Within a system like Etsy, you must figure that there many competitors offering handmade products similar to yours in function and appeal. What determines a winning pricing strategy is the feedback you get, the presentation of your store, and the level of engagement you foster between you and your prospective buyer.

In general, place a premium on a handful of your work, such as pieces that are of higher quality. Also maintain an average price range for the majority of your products. It's beneficial to have a few inexpensive items as well, since people always love a good bargain. This pricing structure increases the likelihood of good sales.

Copyrights & Intellectual Property

This is kind of a tricky area, and Etsy has its own policies and guidelines for you to learn about how copyright laws and intellectual property rights affect you. Since you are putting your work online for the world to see (and potentially copy), you should know your rights. You should also be aware that copyright infringement of other's work will result in listings being removed, and if the violation is severe, it could result in your shop being closed. There is an appeal process if you feel that you were wronged in any way, but be aware of the dangers of copyright infringement.

Etsy has a whole page on its website dedicated to copyright and intellectual property information and guidance. It is helpful because it is written in language that's easy to understand and useful to you as you get started. Take some time and familiarize yourself with the laws and rights surrounding these two areas, so you know how you will be protected if you feel your rights have been violated.

CHAPTER FOUR

Understanding The Marketplace

To make a significant profit selling your items, you should always keep your customer base in mind. It is important that you regularly ask yourself, "Are people going to want to buy my product?" The products you offer should be a cross between what you can provide and what the typical Etsy customer wants. It is also crucial to bear in mind where you stack up against the competition. These factors figure significantly on how your business unfolds and expands.

What Does the Typical Etsy Customer Want?

The needs of an Etsy customer are not limited to the functionality of the product. A hair tie is a hair tie, but why would someone choose to buy it on Etsy for three times the cost of a hair tie at their local drug store? The answer is because there is an added value to the products found on Etsy. The products at Etsy are unique, handmade and one-of-a-kind. They offer a sense character and individuality that a local drugstore can't provide. Your product needs to be perceived this way.

You need to sell a product where individuality and passion meet. This is easy enough to achieve for those of you who have the ability to make bangles or earrings out of twisted metals, but what about the rest of us? Don't worry; there are alternative ways of making money on Etsy. One of these ways is selling items under the vintage category. Look for something that a customer loves. For those of you who may not be armed with artistic skill, that desire to see your customers satisfied is going to get you a long way in succeeding on Etsy.

Marketing

Begin to look at products beyond just an offering that serves a singular purpose. A dog blanket is not an item that just serves to keep a dog warm; instead, it is a handmade sweater to keep the pet you love warm and looking great. Now, a simple dog blanket has been turned into an act of love as well as a fashion statement. Take time to read between the lines to determine what you're actually selling. It may be something intangible. In another way to view marketing, think about car brands. A person doesn't just buy a car, they buy the brand it represents. It's like choosing between a Lincoln and a Land Rover; both are cars and get you places, but one brand says something entirely different from the other. The same marketing principles apply to your product on Etsy. You have the opportunity to define your product in any way you want. It's not just a shop window, it's a window into the personality of the seller and the whims of the consumer.

Your product needs to occupy a range, but it should be a range that has an identity. When you cater to a large clientele, you should customize your product so that it's highly unique and more desirable. Essentially, what you're creating is a brand; this brand ultimately takes on a life of its own. This is what makes a profitable difference between you and someone else on Etsy.

Promotion

You may get some form of traffic just putting up a store on Etsy . Most likely this traffic will result in impulse buys. This is fine, but there are things you can do to increase traffic and get sales from customers who view your shop. In order to take full advantage of being on Etsy, you should promote your store. The first step is to define your audience and present yourself to that specific audience. For example, say that your Etsy store features canvas artwork that you paint yourself. It would be great self-promotion to make flyers displaying your work and including a link to your Etsy site. Hang your flyers in your local artisan shop, coffee house, or craft fair.

Another promotional strategy is to select a few key bloggers, either video or written. They should be prominent in the niche area you occupy, but not your competitors on Etsy. If these bloggers have websites that reviews and research products, this is a good way to promote your unique brand of products. Contact them to see if they would like to feature you as a guest blogger. Send them a free sample of your product or work. They may be able to write a rave review of your store, as well as link their viewers to to your Etsy store from their blog site.

If you have your own blog or website that gets a lot of traffic, it would be valuable to use that as a promotional platform for your Etsy site. Don't have a blog or website? Start one! Look into sites like Blogger or WordPress. Keep in mind that getting traffic to these will take promotion as well.

Utilizing other social media platforms, such as Facebook, Google+, LinkedIn, Twitter, YouTube, Pinterest, and Instagram, is an excellent way to promote yourself. These sites and applications will allow you to display your work to millions of people all over the world who can instantly click and be directed to your Etsy store. Don't rule out setting up an email list where newsletters or promotional material can be sent directly to interested or past customers. Make sure you use an email that is incorporates your name or your shop name so that you are identifiable with the email. You want your customers to open your email, and you want to be able to greet them personally. This is an opportunity for you to be personal, which is something unique to Etsy.

Another area to look into is search engine marketing ("SEM"). This works by placing banner ads on Google's search engine results page. Have you ever noticed the sponsored ads that show up on the right-hand side of the page after you Google something? Those companies have set up SEM for their products or services. For instance, if your Etsy page features wedding merchandise, you can choose key words like: wedding, event, plaque, engrave, engage, reception hall, etc. Whenever someone searches for those keywords, they will see your ad appear in the sponsored ads in the right side column. When you do this, it costs you nothing for the advertisement; you are only charged when people click on the ad and land on your Etsy page. You can hire a SEM professional or you can do it yourself. Google makes it fairly easy for you to learn the ins and outs of traffic generation, and they also give you statistics necessary to make the right decision. The benefit is that you only pay for the times the advertisement works in your favor. It also gives you the opportunity to direct your advertisement at your target audience.

Part of SEM is search engine optimization ("SEO). Search engine optimization works a little differently than SEM. When you concentrate on SEO, your end goal is to have your Etsy shop show up in a Google search for keywords related to your products. If someone Googles wedding plaques, your goal is to have your Etsy shop appear at least on the first page of Google results (because mostpeople don't look past the first page of their search results). By using SEO techniques and ideas, you can make sure that this happens.. Information about this technique is out there for you to try and improve your results on your own, but SEO professionals can be hired to ensure that you get the best results. Regardless of the route you choose, ensuring that your shop is well advertised is a key component to being successful on Etsy, so be willing to put in the time and energy to get the job done right.

Packaging

There are four aspects to packaging your product that you need to consider. The first is the packaging of the product in the conventional sense. This refers to the product's physical package when it arrives at your customer's front door. If you are shipping something fragile, make sure it is packaged securely with that fragility in mind. The second is to consider how your product will be presented when it is opened. This is your chance to add a little personal touch to your product. Remember that people are shopping on Etsy because they are looking for a personalized, unique product. Consider adding a small handwritten thank you note or tying a little ribbon around the product with your logo attached. If you have business cards, make sure you add one to each package as well. Finally, don't forget to give your customers a way to contact you if they find something amiss with the product. They will be able to contact you through Etsy, but you can add in a note letting them know how much you care about their satisfaction and encouraging them to contact you if they are in the least bit dissatisfied with their purchase. The third aspect of packaging is how you present and pair your products online. For instance, you should display a ring and a bracelet together if they match as a way to possibly increase your potential sales. The fourth has to do with the display of products on the screen. It is important to understand lighting and photography to accurately show the color and scale of the products you are selling. Having one great and all-encompassing primary photo is vital, as it's what initially gets the viewer to click on and ultimately buy your product.

Also consider that your photos will need to give them all the information they need to decide whether or not to purchase the products. In addition to a great, eye-catching primary photo, don't forget to include some nice variation shots. This includes high quality shots from the front, back, sides, and detail shots. The same rules of accurate light and color apply to these images as well. Ensure that the captions to these photographs are brief yet descriptive, clear, and concise. Product description is the way to enter the buyer's heart and place your product above your competitors' products. You want to use short and to the point descriptions while using language that invigorates the buyer. Make sure you are thorough so the buyer isn't left asking themselves questions. For example, if you're selling handmade painted pillows, it would be beneficial to list the following: what material they are made from, the dimensions, the patterns or colors, and details about the fabric's maintenance.

CHAPTER FIVE

Taking Your Etsy Store To The Next Level

Write an Etsy Business Plan

Write a business plan that consolidates all your ideas, from inception to profitability, as well as strategies and alternatives in case unforeseen problems arise. Always be open to the possibility of loss and make sure you have the ability to contend with it.

Sole Proprietorships and DBA

When you start up on Etsy, you begin selling without setting up a company; thus, you are essentially doing so as a sole proprietor. That simply means that you take full responsibility on a personal level for everything in the company, from obligations to rewards. There are no papers to file or approvals to seek. Once you are up and running and you make your first sale, you're there. One thing to remember is that you have to be the only person involved. Because the "sole" in sole proprietor means exactly that – one person. If there are two or more of you, then it falls under a general partnership. If you decide you want to do business under a name other than your own, then you would need to get a "DBA" – a "doing business as" certificate. If your name is Mary Poppins and you want to do business as Pinocchio, you would need to file for a DBA certificate. Each city and state have different requirements. Check your particular location to determine what they are. The process is fairly simple and painless. With regard to a DBA and taxes, the profits and losses will be reflected in your personal taxes with any other incomes that you receive.

General Partnership

A general partnership exists between two or more people who go into business together. A general partnership is as simple to set up as a sole proprietorship and carries similar features. Even taxes are the same, as they flow through the personal income tax of each partner. The difference is that it is advisable to have a partnership agreement between the partners so that there are no misunderstandings down the road. No one intends for these kinds of things to occur, but it is always better be on the safe side. Some things that should be addressed are how profits and costs would be divided and an exit strategy for either of the partners. It is best to have a legal professional draw up the agreement and to do so at the outset, even before you set up a shop at Etsy. If your general partnership is going to be all about Etsy, you also need to make it clear how the accounts will be handled in the event of dissolution of the partnership.

LLC or Inc.

As your business grows, or even before it does, you should consider setting up a full-fledged company. There are numerous benefits to this; you may begin to see these advantages as soon as you start applying for vendor credit and payment terms for supplies. The major difference for setting up a limited liability company ("LLC") versus a general partnership or a sole proprietorship is that it creates a separate entity. From a legal standpoint, a company is not the same as the person who owns it. Imagine you are a shareholder in Microsoft, and the company gets sued. The liability does not pierce the corporate veil, and you would not be personally affected. This is the greatest benefit of being incorporated. If you happen to be sued for product liability or your workers are injured in the shop during production, LLC and corporations offer some personal liability protection, while general partnerships and sole proprietorships do not.

Ideally, you should set up a company as soon as you decide to get involved in a business on Etsy. This would save you the hassle of changing things when you get bigger and busier. The cost to incorporate varies from state to state. The process of incorporating in any of the 50 states is fairly easy and can be handled online. Legal advice on which state and which structure to use is advised. Consult with an attorney and check online or with your state's Department of State for more information and benefits of incorporating in that state.

CHAPTER SIX
Successful & Profitable Long Term

So you've opened your shop, you've made a few products, and you're ready to get started selling. Here is some important advice to make sure you have a successful experience selling on Esty.

Creating Your Listings

There are several important aspects to creating listings for your products. We've already discussed the importance of taking good, quality photos. Next, remember that the title of your item is crucial to attracting people to your shop. The first five words of your title are the most important, because they are seen when people search for products. Take your time and make sure the first five words you choose really accentuate your product and explain exactly what it is.

After a potential customer clicks on the link to your product, they will see your product description. and descriptive. This is your chance to make sure everyone knows all the great features of your product. Take full advantage of the area given to you for the description. Give all the details you can think of that highlight your product without being overly wordy. If it helps, ask other people what they would want to know about your product. You can also search products similar to yours for ideas about the kinds of things you should include in your description.

Keywords are also important to making your listing a success. Etsy allows you a certain number of keywords per listing. Take advantage of all of them. Think of any 1 relevant words that might link customers back to your products. These keywords are the way your products show up during searches. Use more keywords to ensure your products show up more often during searches. For example, if you are making wedding bouquets, don't just use the keywords "wedding" and "bouquet," also use "wedding flowers," "engagement," "flower arrangements," etc. Think of other terms that might be related to your product, and use it as a keyword.

Think Like a Customer

When you first list your items at Etsy, try to put yourself in the shoes of a customer. If it helps, search around other shops and get yourself in the mindset of a customer before you get started. Ask yourself, "What kinds of things do my customers want to know about my product?" Make sure your pictures and product descriptions answer all the questions your customers might have.

What other kinds of things do customers care about? Customers care about what other people are saying. Consider sending free samples to friends or family members, and ask them to write reviews for you or link your products and Esty store on their blog pages with a rave review. Any positive publicity you can get is helpful.

Market Research

You did market research when you first started your Etsy shop and probably again when you determined the prices for your products, but it's important that you continue to do market research even after your products are listed. Market research will give you an idea of what's going on in your particular niche or genre. You'll learn how trends are leaning and how that will affect your sales. It can also affect how you price your items. You may decide to lower the prices of certain items after seeing a trend of similar items selling at a lower price. Mostly, it's just important that you keep up with the market so you are informed and educated about your field. That way, nothing will come as a surprise to you.

Payment Methods

When you first set up your shop, you'll be able to decide what types of payment methods you will accept from your customers. This is based on personal preference and how you would like to be paid; however, the more options you allow, the more customers you can reach. For example, there may be some customers that aren't comfortable giving out their credit card information online. These customers may be more comfortable using PayPal or even a mailing a check. Regardless, you may find that by having more options available, you will sell more products to customers who would have otherwise left your shop empty handed. Etsy has four basic payment methods set up for both sellers and buyers. You can choose to accept one or all of them. Etsy offers Direct Check-out, Check or Money Order, PayPal, and an Other option. Here's a quick breakdown of how Etsy explains those methods. Obviously getting paid is one of the most important parts of the process, so take your time and carefully evaluate each of the payment methods offered by Etsy.

Etsy's Fees

You have probably wondered about whether or not it costs anything to set up and start a shop on Etsy. We've mentioned that opening a shop is free, so how does Etsy make its money? Etsy charges you for every item you list in your shop. The listing fee is $.20 USD per item. The item will be listed for four months in your shop or until it sells. If you choose to re-list it after the four months expire, you'll pay another $.20 USD per item fee. Etsy also charges for every sale you make in your shop. You aren't charged until your items sell, but once they have sold, you will owe Etsy 3.5% of the sale price. These are important numbers to consider when you are setting your prices for various products in your shop. The Etsy pricing calculator discussed earlier factors in these fees, but it is important that you remember them as well, so you're not surprised after the sale of an item.

Use the "About Me" Section

It's important that you spend some time setting up the section that is dedicated to you. This section is where you get to introduce yourself to the world and to your potential customers. Etsy is really all about personalized interactions with people, so don't be afraid to let your customers know a little about the real you. Obviously you don't want to give out too much personal information, but it is crucial that your customers feel like they can connect with you and know a little about the person from whom they are purchasing their products. If you aren't the best with English grammar and punctuation, have a friend or family member help you out. This is the way you get to introduce yourself, and it will be well done and presentable.

Customer Service

This can't be emphasized strongly enough. If you want to have loyal, returning customers, it is extremely important to have excellent customer service. These loyal customers will help to promote your products simply because they were satisfied and happy with their experience. This is free advertising for you, based on just a little extra work. You are responsible for your own customer service. That means you'll need to answer emails, deal with customer support, handle complaints, etc. It isn't the most enjoyable part of the job, but it is important. You won't have a perfect record with your customers, and you should accept that from the first day you open your shop. There will be misunderstandings, bad shipping experiences, or just disappointed customers. The best customer service people know that bad things happen, but they immediately move to rectify the situation. You should work until your customer is satisfied and happy. This may mean a refund, which isn't, of course, ideal, but it may be the best solution. Other options include repairing the item, replacing the item, or giving the customer an Etsy gift card. Whatever you do, making sure your customers are satisfied is the most crucial part of operating a shop.

Etsy's Free Resources

Etsy is available to help you, the seller, be successful; it's the way they make money, too. Because they want to see you be successful, they have provided a variety of free resources that you should take advantage of as a shop owner. Every two weeks, Etsy emails a free newsletter. This newsletter has success stories, tips, guidelines, strategies and ideas to be successful on Etsy. Take the ten minutes to read it through and learn from the advice of those who know best.

Etsy also has a variety of groups and discussion boards on its website. By joining these groups and discussions, you can learn valuable information from top sellers. People post questions and ideas every day that will help you build a successful shop. Browse through the discussions and find those that are most applicable to you and your ideas. After reading through them, contribute, ask questions, give advice or ideas. Don't be afraid to become part of the Etsy community. The more involved you become, the more traffic your shop will see. Etsy also has a great, extensive FAQ section on their website. Even if you don't have a particular question about the website, it's not a bad idea to spend some time on this part of the website. It will give you some valuable information and could answer some questions you didn't even know you had. The last free resource to take advantage of from Etsy is The Seller Handbook. Etsy has created this handbook specifically for you to walk you through the ins and outs of being successful on Etsy.

Offer Deals & Specials

Don't be afraid to offer deals and specials, especially when you are first starting out. Consider offering special promotions to customers who buy more items; for example, free shipping or a discounted rate for multiple purchases (e.g., 10% off for two items, 20% for three items, 30% off for four and up). These types of deals could help customers who may have been hesitant to buy your products perhaps be more willing to take the plunge. You can also offer reward programs or incentives for loyal customers. Create an email list or Facebook page that your loyal customers can subscribe to or "like." Add in specials, such as four-hour coupon codes or one-day specials for those that actively follow you. These customers are more likely to continually check out your shop for new items or items that they love if you are sending them emails every couple weeks or if they are following you on Facebook.

Offering deals and updating subscribers is more work, but it's work worth doing. By spending the time to create an email newsletter about new products or specials coming up, you willll attract more traffic to your shop. The same applies to continually updating your Facebook page. When people see your updates on their newsfeeds, they will remember to go shopping. Little reminders from you can make all the difference in your profits.

Don't List All Your Items at Once

Even if you have fifteen items ready to list, don't list them all on the first day. This is because when a customer searches for Etsy products, the newest items appear first. Instead, open your shop and list two or three the first day. Then wait a day or two and list a couple more. Over the course of a week or two, list all your items. Obviously you want to get your items listed or you'll never sell anything, but stretching it out over the course of a few weeks can keep you higher on the searches for a longer period of time. This will help get more traffic to your store in the first few weeks you are open.

Be Patient

It's important that you be patient with your success. Rome wasn't built in a day, and your shop won't become successful overnight either. Give it time to gain popularity. It isn't always easy to be patient, but by doing the things outlined in this book, you will have loyal and returning customers, who will help you become successful.

Have Fun

Probably the most important part of opening and watching your Etsy shop grow is having fun. It's essential to have a good time and remember that there will be ups and downs with your sales. Hopefully, you are doing something that you love and have turned a hobby into a business. Continue to enjoy what you are doing regardless of the sales and dollar signs coming into the bank. Have fun, and it will help ensure that you feel successful.

CHAPTER SEVEN

Case Studies of Etsy Powersellers

Wondering if you can make it big on Etsy? It is highly possible, particularly when you combine passion, dedication, determination, and perseverance. Don't be discouraged if you are not making enough sales during your first month. As you learn the ins and outs of the Etsy market, you will discover that you can come up with your own unique brand that people will appreciate and keep coming back for more. Learn from the following Etsy Powersellers on how they have made a mark in the Etsy world, and how you can make a difference as well.

Etsy Powerseller Profile #1 :

The Black Apple by Emily Winfield Martin

For those in the creative visual arts field, observing how The Black Apple made it big on Etsy is worth taking note. With 465 average sales per month and an average monthly revenue of $7,400, Ms. Martin has been carving a sustainable living out of selling on Etsy. Note that Black Apple is not just bounded by selling activities on Etsy, but it also sells work in other places like licensing artwork. The Black Apple shop has the following key qualities:

- **Distinctive Style and Brand** : Her imaginative and whimsical artwork make any art lover heart's melt. Her prints are worthy collectibles. To achieve a "collectible" status, there has to be a certain quality in the work that makes it special and highly sought after.

- **Variety of Products on Offer** : The Black Apple shop offers not just art prints, but also books, postcards, notebooks, pins, magnets, and so much more. She also offers different sizes for her prints, as well as print sets for those who want to collect.

- **Online Presence** : The artist has her own website, as well as a blog for her online shop. She also has thousands of Twitter followers that admire her work and keep tabs on her latest creations. With over 48,989 sales, 61,366 admirers, and thousands of positive reviews, the Black Apple has come a long way and it is still going strong.

Etsy Powerseller Profile #2 :

Zen Threads

Sales of Zen Threads are close to a million dollars, and this is because they have a unique and eco-friendly way of creating their products. They have a refreshing twist to the usual t-shirts, which is inspired by nature, oddities, and the artists' home state. Their products are absolutely affordable and wearable works of art. They have 775 average sales per month with an average monthly revenue of $15,750. That is certainly outstanding for a shop that sells t-shirts online, yet they are not just selling t-shirts; they are selling products made with love and respect for nature. What makes their products sell so well are the following:

- **Irresistible and Wearable Designs** : Just by looking at their shop front, you will feel like buying everything in one shot. Their designs are given careful consideration, so any wearer would be proud to use them. Beauty and functionality make a powerful combination on their products.

- **Eco-friendly Production Process** : All of their products are hand printed and eco-friendly. They use an earth-friendly photo-emulsion process on the most comfortable garments they can procure. Their t-shirts are made in the U.S. and are sweatshop-free. Socially responsible and environmentally friendly operations make this brand an absolute winner.

Etsy Powerseller Profile #3 :

Three Bird Nest

Who would have thought that selling headbands would earn you thousands of dollars per month? Three Bird Nest has 2,300 average sales per month and earns an average monthly revenue of $65,000! Their products sell like hotcakes, and there's no stopping them. This goes to show that finding your market and making the most out of it will definitely make you successful in the world of Etsy. The following is what makes Three Bird Nest so successful:

- **Variety and Functionality** : What makes their products sell so well is the fact that they offer a lot of variety and designs. They don't offer products that will satisfy you with owning just one type; you will want to buy several for different purposes, seasons, and uses. Their accessories make you want to buy more than one, as a treat to yourself or as gifts to your BFFs.

- **Great Product Presentations** : All of their product photos are absolutely eye-candy, which will make anyone click that "buy" button and yearn to look as good as their photographs. There's a lot of style in their product images that are good enough to become spreads in a fashion magazine. This shows you have to give your best in your product photographs, as it can make or break your selling endeavors.

CONCLUSION

If you are just beginning your journey in e-commerce or are
a seasoned veteran, I hope this book was helpful and informative
for you. I am confident that when you combine the knowledge and
strategies presented in this book with the determination and drive to
succeed,anyone will be able to cash in on the Etsy goldrush. The next
step is to put these strategies into action. It is time for you to test your
newly acquired knowledge. Remember that knowledge without action
will amount to nothing. It is only when the two are combined that
success will be achieved.

I want to thank you for reading this book and I sincerely hope
that you received value from it.

ABOUT THE AUTHOR

My name is Devon Wilcox and I am an entrepreneur, life coach and father. I'm also the author of several personal finance, money management and wealth acquisition books. Thank you for checking out my stuff.

As far back as I can remember, I've had a drive within me to make money; starting from a small scale landscaping business I began when I was 14 to owning multiple franchise locations by the time I was 33. I've been motivated my whole life to never allow myself to be a part of the "rat race" and spend day after day stuck in a 9-5 job that I simply did not care about. When I was 18 years old, I had a crystallizing moment where I looked in the mirror and promised to myself that I would always be in control of my financial life and never be a slave to a paycheck. I have since kept that promise, and today can proudly say that I have zero debt, a positive balance sheet, and a happy, stress-free life.

Many of the methods I have implemented to accumulate my wealth are often viewed as "non-conventional" and "unsustainable." I'm here to tell you that those are simply the statements of non-believers, of lazy people, of sheep. The truth is that there are several methods to generate income, both passively and actively, that do not involve waking up and going to a job you hate every day. Surprising, right? Unfortunately, most people settle and choose to live paycheck to paycheck, constantly moments away from a financial meltdown, never attempting to create long-term wealth.

My goal is simple; share with you the numerous proven methods that I, and the hundreds of individuals I have coached, have used to achieve financial freedom. I promise that my books will open your eyes to new ways to make money that have never crossed your mind previously. Your determination, along with the step-by-step guides provided in my books, will be your blueprint to a life free of debt and full of wealth.

PREVIEW OF

eBay Business For Beginners:
Exactly How I Made A Six Figure Income With My eBay Business, And
Why It Is Easier Than You Think!

By : Devon Wilcox

Chapter 1 : Introduction to eBay – Starting With The Basics

When the economy is down, it seems that everyone is interested in ways to make some extra cash. The Internet is flush with "work at home" prospects. Some are legitimate, and some are merely scams or multilevel marketing schemes requireing you to recruit members or additional sales people and sell products to your friends and family. However, there is one certain strategy that you can use to make some extra cash from home, or even build a successful business that can provide reliable income: selling goods on eBay. While some people are under the impression that the eBay ship has already sailed, so to speak, there are still plenty of opportunities to cash in selling goods online with eBay's platform, or even to build a successful eBay-based business. Whether you are looking to earn some extra spending cash, pay for a family vacation, or build a full-time, regular income-earning business, eBay remains one of the easiest ways to accomplish your goal.

History Tidbits about eBay

In 1995, just when the Internet was starting to take off, a 28-year-old software designer by the name of Pierre Omidyar launched a website he called AuctionWeb. Legend says that he created the website as an online trading forum for his girlfriend to easily trade PEZ™ dispensers, a number of which she had recently bought while on vacation in Europe. The AuctionWeb site was fairly rudimentary but functional. PEZ™ dispensers notwithstanding, Omidyar wanted to revolutionize the marketplace by giving buyers and sellers greater and easier access to each other and their products. His goal was to give everyone in the world admission to a single online marketplace, a revolutionary idea that completely leveled the playing field of commerce. The first successful auction was for, believe it or not, a broken laser pointer! Omidyar contacted the winning bidder just to confirm that the bidder understood that the laser pointer was, in fact, broken. As a testament to what would become one of the reasons why eBay has been so successful, Omidyar found out that the man actually collected broken laser pointers. The lesson was: no matter what you have to sell, or how odd it is, there may actually be someone out there that who really wants it. Within about a week of starting AuctionWeb, the website had sold a set of Marky Mark underwear for $400, a Toyota for $3200, and a Superman lunchbox for $22. Yes, you can buy and sell just about anything (legal) on eBay!

The eBay name came from an abbreviation of Echo Bay, which had already been taken as a domain name when Omidyar tried to register it. eBay was originally a parent company for AuctionWeb and two of Omidyar's other internet based companies. Omidyar changed both the platform design and the name from AuctionWeb to eBay in 1997, giving the website a more interactive and colorful design and logo.

With hundreds of millions of items for sale at any given time, eBay has become the largest online marketplace in the world. One can find just about anything for sale - from toys, jewelry, art, crafts, collectibles, tools, electronics, automobiles, real estate, aircraft, sporting event and entertainment event tickets, advertising space (one guy made over $30,000 for advertising space on his forehead) and much, much more. A Gulfstream II jet that sold in 2001 for $4.9 million is among the most expensive items sold on eBay. Items can be listed for sale at auction or with a fixed "buy it now" price, which ends an auction early with or without a reserve or minimum price. Items can even be sold for best offer or second chance offer. By 2010, the fixed price sales had exceeded the auction sales.

In today's world of mobile technology, mobile e-commerce is also becoming increasingly popular. By 2010, eBay users were purchasing an item using an eBay mobile app approximately every two seconds. Hundreds of millions of dollars were being exchanged by using the mobile app yearly since 2010, including big ticket items like a Lamborghini for nearly $140,000 and a Piper Malibu airplane for $265,000. eBay mobile apps not only make it easy to buy, they make it easy to sell.

eBay also integrated an app called Red Laser into its own apps so users can actually scan a product's bar code with the camera on their mobile device. If the app recognizes the product code, it will tell the user whether or not that item is for sale on eBay. It will also list current and past auctions for that product with the option of creating a new listing to sell it. The same app that is used to read product bar codes can also read shipment tracking number bar codes. This feature gives eBay sellers the ability to scan a UPS, FedEx or US Postal Service shipping label to directly upload shipment and tracking information for a sold item. This is a handy feature, given some of the long tracking numbers that a seller would otherwise have to manually type in to show that an item has been shipped.

In addition to using bar codes, mobile apps give users an easy way to create new listings from scratch or by searching active or closed eBay listings and using a "sell one like this" feature. Photos can be uploaded from a mobile device by choosing existing photos or by taking new photos that the app uploads directly without having to save them to your device. The listing process is streamlined in the mobile apps and is very easy to complete. We will examine the details and techniques for creating listings in Chapter 3.

eBay and Paypal Merger

In 2002, eBay purchased PayPal, the primary service used by eBay buyers and sellers (also called eBayers) for transferring funds and making payments for purchases. With a PayPal account, eBayers can quickly and easily pay for goods and receive payment from buyers. A PayPal account can be funded by mailing a check, by making a transfer from a credit or debit card, or by making a transfer from a bank account. Funds can also be transferred from a PayPal account to a checking account, or can be mailed to an account holder in the form of a check. While eBay purchases can be made by credit card and other forms of payment, PayPal is the fastest and easiest method. Transactions are protected by PayPal, which offers a dispute resolution service in addition to the service offered by eBay. In addition to the seller fees that eBay charges to sellers, PayPal charges its own fees to account holders for making transactions. Fees are based on a percentage of the transaction amount and are fairly reasonable and nominal. In the case that a transaction is reversed, fees are refunded.

While there are certainly a lot of good features offered by both eBay and PayPal, they are both very large companies and as a result. customer service can suffer. Contacting either company with complaints outside of the buyer and seller resolution system can be very difficult and unsatisfying. Disputing a final resolution decision can be impossible, and dispute resolutions decided by either PayPal or eBay in the favor of one party or another are not always fair. Experienced eBayers know and accept this as a part of doing business, and either find look for ways to work around it or deal with it as one of the costs of running a business.

How eBay works

eBayers use a system of providing feedback in order to rate each other and give other eBayers a way of measuring confidence in each other. The eBay feedback system certainly has its flaws and can seem to be one sided in favor of the buyers. However, it does a pretty good job of holding sellers accountable in a number of areas including quality (is the item as described?), communication, and shipping (both cost of shipping and speed of shipping) by allowing buyers to give sellers numerically based ratings that are tracked, averaged, and made public for other buyers to see. Sellers are able to both respond to buyer feedback and leave limited comments as feedback for buyers.

eBay makes money by charging fees to sellers. The eBay fee structure can be confusing, and sellers need to be aware and keep track of the fees so that the cost of sales doesn't add up and eat anticipated profits. Most of eBay's fees are assessed as a final value fee, which is a percentage of the final selling price of an item. Fee schedules vary for automobile listings, real estate listings, eBay classified ads, eBay Store subscribers, and business and industrial categories. There are standard listing (insertion) fees in addition to final value fees, but eBay often runs promotions that waive these fees for items that are listed while the promotion is running. One thing to be aware of is that sellers need to notify eBay in the case that a buyer does not pay for an item in order to get fees refunded. In some cases, like motor vehicle listings, final value fees may not be refunded even when a buyer does not pay, so sellers need to be diligent when deciding whether or not to accept a winning bid for certain auctions, and in specifying bidder qualifications in the terms of an auction. eBay's fee schedule can be found at http://pages. ebay.com/help/sell/fees.html

Once an item has been sold on eBay, a buyer generally has a few days to make the payment for the purchase. Depending on the seller's preferences, a payment may be made using any one of a number of available options. As we mentioned earlier, PayPal is one of the easiest and safest methods, though funds are not made available for up to several days while a new seller builds a reputation on eBay. Once an item has been sold and paid for, the seller is notified by email and is advised to ship the item.

When a seller has established a history of reliably shipping items soon after purchases, the PayPal funds will be available sooner. Additional methods include credit card, check, payment in person for local pick up items, plus a number of other online payment services. A seller may send a buyer an invoice that includes the winning bid price plus shipping and handling costs, or if all additional costs have been predetermined, the buyer can use a pay now feature without waiting for an invoice.

eBay also has additional tools for sellers that simplify the selling and shipping process. When a seller lists an item, the seller may choose a method of shipping to offer to buyers. The seller could choose to offer more than one shipping method, ranging from economy options to expedited options, including a courier service. Buyers are able to choose which option the seller will use at the end of the auction or upon purchasing an item. Once a seller has sold an item and is ready to ship it, the seller has the option of shipping it outside of eBay and uploading shipping information, such as the shipping service or carrier and the tracking number. The seller may also use eBay's own shipping system. eBay's shipping system gives sellers the opportunity to select from a number of different carriers like the U.S. Postal Service, UPS or FedEx, and to select from a number of available services from each carrier. Services may include options like standard ground transportation, expedited ground transportation, standard air, overnight air, and in some cases, even same day delivery. The system allows a seller to purchase postage or shipping labels with funds from a PayPal account or a credit card, after which labels or postage can be printed on a home computer printer and affixed to a package for shipping. When a seller uses the eBay shipping system, all tracking information is automatically uploaded into the eBay record for a sale, enabling the buyer to access it and track the shipment. Items can also be shipped by taking them to a postal, FedEx or UPS location. Tracking information can be manually entered on the website or labels can be scanned using a mobile app. Sellers are advised to track shipments in order to stay informed as to when the final phase of an eBay purchase - the feedback phase - should start.

At the end of all transactions, eBay uses a unique feedback system as a means of rating both sellers and buyers. The system allows buyers to give a rating to a seller that judges the overall selling experience so that other buyers can determine whether or not they want to bid on the seller's items. The rating system is based on a numerical average of a score from one to five stars in four different categories. The categories include whether the item received was as described in the eBay listing, whether or not the shipping and handling charges were reasonable, how well the seller communicated with the buyer, and how quickly the item was shipped after the auction ended. Sellers are only given the opportunity to either leave positive feedback or no feedback for buyers, and to leave comments in response to buyer feedback. The eBay feedback system has been criticized as favoring buyers and being unfair to sellers, so successful sellers pay very close attention to buyer feedback and take all possible steps to maintain good ratings.

While buyers may overlook poor seller ratings, eBay itself does not, punishing sellers with account restrictions when ratings fall below eBay standards. It is important to keep in mind that a seller rating can be deceiving, which is why buyers sometimes overlook or disregard low ratings. Ratings are given as a percentage, similar to a test score. What is not similar is that a 95% test score is very good, while a 95% eBay seller rating is not. eBay even considers a score as high as 98% to be poor! Sellers should strive for a rating of at least 99%. This is accomplished by immediately responding to buyer and even bidder questions, shipping quickly and within eBay's recommended timeframe, offering multiple shipping options that include both economy and expedited means, packing items well, charging no more than ten or fifteen percent more than actual shipping cost, and writing a very good description with quality photos in listings. We will discuss these strategies further in Chapters 3, 4 and 5.

This concludes our overview of eBay and the basics of how it operates. In the next chapter we will discuss what is required to set up a seller account with eBay and the PayPal account that eBay requires all sellers to have.

Chapter 2 : First Step To Creating Your eBay Business

In order to sell goods on eBay you will, of course, need an eBay seller account. Having a seller account simply means setting up an eBay account that you use to sell things. You don't do anything special to set up a seller account as opposed to a bidding account; they are actually the same account. The difference is that in order to sell goods on eBay you will need a means to pay eBay fees to keep the account in good standing, and you need to have a PayPal account. eBay has been criticized for the PayPal requirement, especially in light of the fact that eBay now owns PayPal. Some see the requirement as a means for eBay to profit more by forcing sellers to use PayPal, which charges transaction fees in addition to the fees charged by eBay. Some also see the PayPal requirement as another way for eBay to favor buyers if a transaction goes wrong, resulting in a dispute. PayPal will almost always favor a buyer in such a dispute, even when the seller can provide strong evidence to support the seller's side of the disagreement. One example of this practice is in the case when a buyer reports a package received without its contents or with damaged contents. PayPal generally automatically refunds the buyer from the seller's account without requiring the buyer to return the package to the seller. There are ways for sellers to mitigate such risks, and we will discuss them in Chapter 3.

Setting up a basic eBay account is fairly simple and does not take long. In order to get started on eBay, you will need an email account. It is recommended that sellers set up a separate account that is specifically used for selling goods on eBay, using a provider such as gmail.com, hotmail.com or msn.com (now outlook.com) or yahoo.com. An email account can easily be set up with any of these providers, and is most easily done when you already have another email account that the provider can send an activation email to. When setting up your email account, use an email address that is catchy, easy to remember and that makes good sense to use, keeping in mind that you are essentially setting up a business email address. It should not be offensive, vulgar or silly. You should look and sound professional. This email address will also be your login and screen name on your eBay account. Make sure you provide accurate information when opening the email account, such as your name, birthday and phone number. eBay frowns upon accounts that are set up with vague or false information as do email providers. The last thing you want to happen is to for eBay or PayPal to suspend your account because of conflicting or unverifiable information.

Once you have a valid email address, you are now ready to set up an eBay account. Go to the eBay website and look for the "Login/ Register" link in the upper right hand corner of the web page, and click on the "Register" link. In order to set up your account, you will also need a physical address, your name and phone number, and some other personal information. You will be given the option to have eBay choose a screen name (nickname) for you or you can choose your own, but be aware that with the millions of eBay users out there the name you might choose is likely to have already been taken. This is why it is a good idea to use your email address or some logical extension or variation of it. You will also need to choose a password that meets eBay's standards for security; choose wisely and consider changing it regularly, as you should treat all information you provide to be only as secure as your password. Once you have completed the registration process, having confirmed that you are 18 years of age or older and that you agree to eBay's terms and conditions, eBay will email you a confirmation link. Follow the instructions in the confirmation email to finish the account registration process.

Now that you have a basic eBay account, you will need to open a PayPal account. Your PayPal account will allow you to quickly and easily send and receive payments for eBay items without having to continuously enter credit card and billing information or wait for checks and money orders from buyers. There will be a "Sign Up for PayPal" link on the eBay confirmation page that will take you to PayPal's account registration page. You can use that link, or you can go directly to the PayPal website. However, it is recommended that you use the PayPal link from eBay's website, as this will automatically link your PayPal account to your eBay account.

The PayPal registration process is similar to the eBay registration process: easy and simple. You will also need a credit card or a checking account to link to your PayPal account, either of which will be used to verify your identity and to provide a means of funding your PayPal account. Linking a checking account to your PayPal account will also give you an easy means of withdrawing funds from PayPal. You also have the option of adding a savings account in lieu of a checking account. PayPal will verify your account by making one or more small deposits into your bank account after which you will need to log into PayPal and confirm the amounts that were deposited. Linking a bank account to your PayPal account will also verify your PayPal account, which removes certain restrictions such as limitations on amounts that you can withdraw. To complete the PayPal account registration process, just follow the instructions provided by PayPal and you will be ready to fund your account.

The Basics of Building Up Your Account

Before you begin selling with an active eBay account, you will need to make a few purchases to build a history with eBay and to get some feedback. With hundreds of millions of items listed on eBay at any given time, it won't be hard to find something you want or need. Log into your eBay account and explore the site. You can take some time browsing through the many different categories, or you can use eBay's search engine to search for specific products that may interest you. As you familiarize yourself with the search engine, you will find that you can narrow the search results by selecting any of a number of criteria that apply. You can refine your search by a specific category (eBay Motors, cell phones and accessories, clothing, consumer electronics, etc), by condition (new, used, etc.), by buying format (auction, buy it now, accepts offers) and many more.

Your first several purchases should be for items priced no higher than $10 or so. To bid, select an item that is listed as an auction and follow eBay's instructions for entering and confirming a maximum bid. Once you have done this, eBay will automatically send you confirmation emails each time the current bid is increased until your maximum bid is reached. As other bidders bid higher amounts, eBay will automatically enter new bids for you at specific bid increments until your maximum bid is reached, at which time eBay will let you know so that you can raise your bid if you want. You can also watch the auction in real time on the website. The listing will show the remaining time for the auction and will countdown by day, then hour, then minute and finally seconds right up to the end of the auction. If you find an item that is listed with a buy it now price, you may find it more convenient to use that feature rather than waiting through the auction process. You may find that you have one or more questions about an item, either before or after bidding on it. Questions can be submitted to sellers through eBay's messaging system by using the "Contact Seller" link in a listing. Buyers and sellers can communicate in writing; messages are sent through eBay to personal email accounts. You can send photos or even communicate by video. If you win the auction, eBay will notify you by email, so you can pay for the item and select a shipping option.

Upon winning an auction, buy it now or best offer, your eBay home page will display the item in a section of your page that is used to keep track of items purchased or won. You will also see that there are folders for items that you are bidding on, have bid on but not won, and even items you have looked at or searched for recently. When you begin selling, eBay will populate folders with your listings that are selling (active listings), and sold and unsold (ended listings that did not sell) listings as well. When paying for a won item, you may be asked to choose a payment method and a shipping option, although some sellers may only offer PayPal as a means of payment and only one means of shipping. Follow eBay's instructions for payment and confirmation of shipping method (don't forget to double check your delivery address), and await notification of shipment from the seller. Once your item ships you can track the shipment by using the tracking information that the shipper entered into eBay. Not all sellers use shipment methods that include tracking information, but as a buyer you can decide whether or not that is important to you before bidding.

Once you have completed a purchase and your item has been delivered, you should log into eBay and leave feedback for the seller. Leaving feedback is voluntary but encouraged, as long as it is honest and reasonable. You can leave feedback by clicking on the feedback link on your "My eBay" page or by visiting the eBay feedback forum. As a buyer, you will be asked to leave a one to five star rating for the seller in each of the aforementioned categories. You may also leave a detailed seller rating and comments for or about the seller. Be fair and encourage the seller to leave positive feedback for you. Sometimes sellers are overwhelmed and forget to leave feedback for buyers, so don't be shy and be sure to send the seller a reminder if necessary. Building a good buyer reputation is helpful and will be an encouragement to prospective buyers when you become a seller.

Now that you have some buying experience and a history of positive feedback, you can start making money yourself by opening a seller account. As we mentioned before, a seller account is not really a separate account; it's more of an upgrade to your existing account. First you will want to verify that the personal information eBay has on file for you is correct. You can do this by logging in to your eBay account and clicking the "My eBay" link in the upper right hand corner of your eBay page. Click the "Account" link from the drop down menu, and then click "Personal Information." Verify that your name, address, phone number and other information is correct and edit as necessary. Next you will need to set up a payment method for eBay fees and eBay's Money Back Guarantee. eBay will use this payment method to automatically pay fees and to give refunds to qualifying buyers in case a transaction goes sour. The aforementioned steps will qualify you to sell on eBay, but you will also want to make sure that you are PayPal Verified as well, because that will enable you to sell more freely on eBay. To become PayPal Verified, you will need to click the appropriate link either from your eBay page or your PayPal page and follow the instructions for linking a bank account to your PayPal account. Now you are ready to list your first item for sale!

Listing an item is easy, but it should be done diligently and with as much detail as needed to attract and inform buyers. We will examine the listing process in detail in Chapters 3 and 4.

MORE BY DEVON

Stock Trading Strategies For Beginners

Simple Stock Trading Strategies For Maximum Profits

Visit: http://bit.ly/stock_trading_rich

Day Trading For Beginners

How To Quit Your Job And Get Rich Day Trading

Visit: http://bit.ly/day_trading

Options Trading For Beginners

How To Get Rich With Stock Options Trading

Visit: http://bit.ly/optionsrich

Bitcoin Beginner's Guide

Everything You Need To Know To Become Rich With Bitcoins

Visit: http://bit.ly/bitcoinrich

Couponing For Beginners

How to Save Thousands A Year Couponing

Visit: http://bit.ly/save_coupons

Printed in Great Britain
by Amazon.co.uk, Ltd.,
Marston Gate.